MW01420183

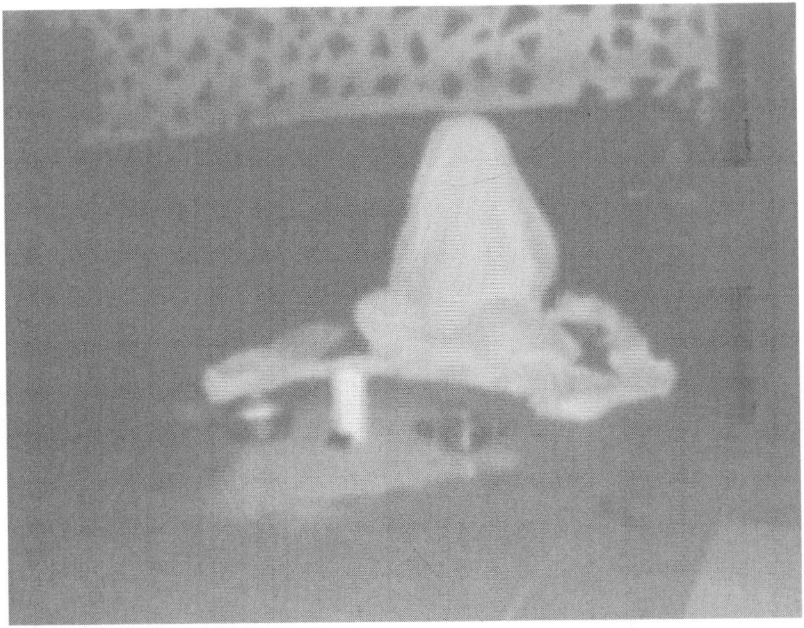

(ghost gestures)

performance writing

Gabrielle Civil

Gold Line Press

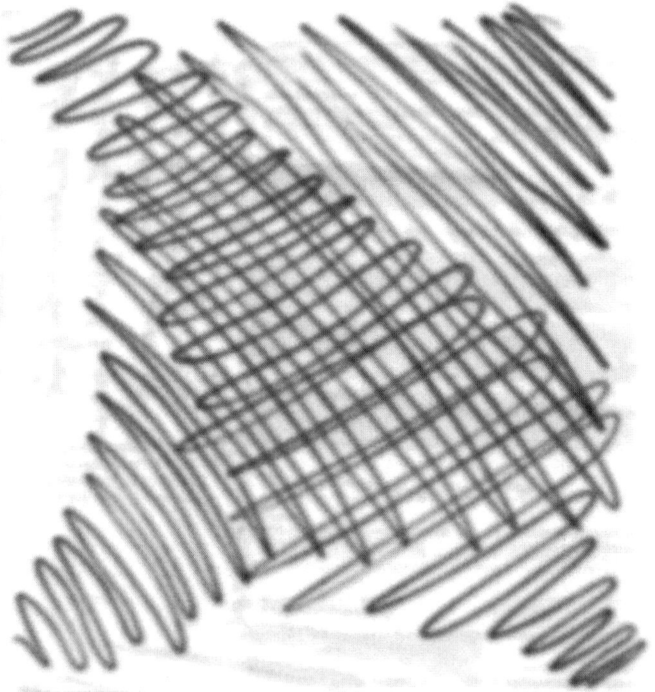

Copyright© 2021 by Gabrielle Civil
All rights reserved

Cover and book design: Kenji Liu
Published: Gold Line Press
http://goldlinepress.com
Gold Line titles are distributed by Small Press Distribution
This title is also available for purchase directly from the publisher
www.spdbooks.org / 800.869.7553

Library of Congress Cataloging-in-Publication Data
(*ghost gestures*) / Gabrielle Civil
Library of Congress Control Number 2021932697
Civil, Gabrielle
ISBN 978-1-938900-38-9

FIRST EDITION

Table of Contents

(Dakar)   3

the doll

Muño (fantasia de la Negrita)   7

(Montreal)   28

the queen

Anacaona   46

(Detroit)   65

the ghost

ghost/ gesture   70

Welcome to haunting . . .

Meditations on cities mark diaspora wanderings.

Performance texts offer past projections, transcriptions, and scores.

"In the third-world cosmology as I perceive it, reality is not already constituted by my literary predecessors in Western culture. If my work is to confront a reality unlike that received reality of the West, it must centralize and animate information discredited by the West . . . information held by discredited people, information dismissed as 'lore' or 'gossip' or 'magic' or sentiment."
—Toni Morrison
The Source of Self-Regard

(Dakar: Black Women Dancing in Mirrors)

What do they see there? Dancing with their backs to the crowd, their faces absorbed in reflections. Women of Dakar dancing in mirrors, wearing tight, embroidered jeans, or short miniskirts with tall boots. Wearing thick lipstick, powder, and blush. Wearing wigs or weaves. Wearing elaborate braids. Women of Dakar, so stunning in their beauty, their style, their dark brown skin, their touch of haughtiness. Their gestures so precise, they are almost ceremonial.

A certain thrust, a powerful turn of the hip, done as if effort was no expense. And yet, that's not true. Try to do it. Try to stand there and roll your hips, slowly, surely, with control, with beauty, looking only into your own eyes. And then when the song is right—when Youssou N'Dour starts to wail—and it's 3 AM and everyone is finally there, gleaming, preening, steady cool, do it more, not necessarily faster but deeper, not necessarily harder but smoother. See the Women of Dakar, dancing in mirrors, dip their knees open in time. See how a hand swims up, a head turns, catches a glimpse of itself somewhere else. Catches a glimpse maybe of something else. Catches a glimpse of you, a country cousin.

Oumar has brought me here.
Says: if you came back here, you could learn Wolof
just like that! And when you wear the right clothes,
you could be one of us.
You are already one of us.

Across the water, your people were taken,
but we have the same ancestors, the same blood.
And you could even take one of our names.
My last name is Diaw.
Now, you are Gabrielle Diaw.
>   Not so fast.
>   Not so easy.
>   That is not my name.

My gestures, larger, more expressionistic. My dancing takes up more space, holds my body in its own way. The Women in Dakar see themselves dancing in mirrors and they see me too. I know because when I dance, I can't see their faces, but spy their reflections, winking, smirking, laughing back at me.

>   I dance with Oumar, but I don't dance for him.
>   I dance for the crowd, the people on the floor.
>   I dance for the wail and the throb of sound.
>   I dance for these women dancing in mirrors.
>   I try to impress them, but they pay me no mind.
>   I dance for the mirrors, to get inside reflections.
>   I dance for these women. I want them to see me.
>   I want their pulsing ease and belonging.
>   I want them to see me in mirrors dancing.
>   I want to see myself in their reflections.
>   I dance for black women dancing in mirrors.

These women, haunting, hovering at the corner of my eye.

the doll

Muño *(fantasía de la negrita)*

full moon.
    a summoning.
        I become la Negrita
            and reveal
                her secret life.

The doll was small, about a foot long, with a cloth body and a 1920s-style, plastic Kewpie face. She was pitch-black like the new moon. Her arms widespread without hands or fingers. Her legs ended in red booties with white polka dots matching her head scarf and dress. The head scarf was a crown of glory, reminiscent of slave head rags, Orisha head wraps, African headdresses, and folded butterfly wings. The dress, made of rough cloth, was high-necked, long, and trimmed in white lace. She wore iridescent powder blue eye shadow, bright red rouge on puffed cheeks, and a red-lipsticked mouth, pursed and ready to kiss or gasp or giggle or blow. She looked like a *mammy* but she wasn't. She was a mix of 19th century servitude and 20th century glamour. Her hair was sculpted plastic, meant to look pulled back straight (it certainly wasn't kinky) beneath her scarf. Only one raised plastic curl lifted up on the center of her forehead. Her eyes were painted white with brown irises and black centers. Spidery eyelashes added incongruous feminine allure. Sweet and happy, familiar and strange, she was supposedly meant for children but was given to me by an art historian friend who knew my predilections. But how could someone give you back yourself?

mammy
1. a pernicious figure in United States popular culture
2. a fat black woman, simple, servile, and asexual, usually depicted in a red and white dress, head scarf, and apron (note: some *negrita* dolls in Mexico come with aprons as well)
3. Scarlett O'Hara's maidservant in *Gone with the Wind*
4. a stereotype conceived in the nineteenth century to make the omnipresence of defenseless black domestics in white households seem less sexually threatening (*because who could be attracted to that?*)
5. a figure to cover prevalent sexual oppression of black women
6. a black woman who exists only to serve, entertain, flatter, caretake, and console whites; known for being especially loving to her white charges and especially evil to her own children (see Mrs. Breedlove in *The Bluest Eye*)
7. a historical figure that still haunts contemporary consciousness (*and mine*)—e.g. Aunt Jemima wearing a lovely strand of pearls
8. a harmless black woman figure who exists only to love you (*what a doll!*)

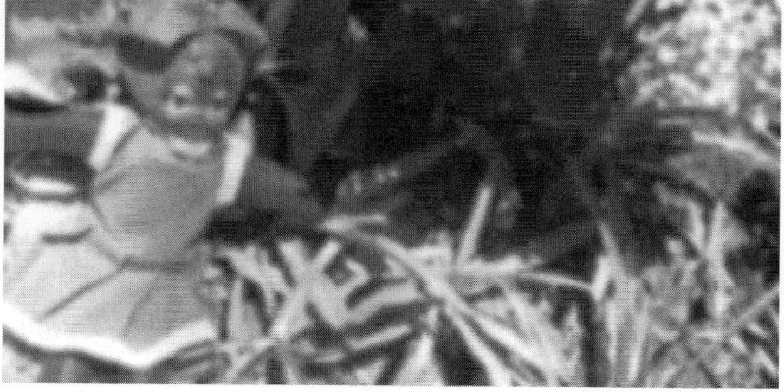

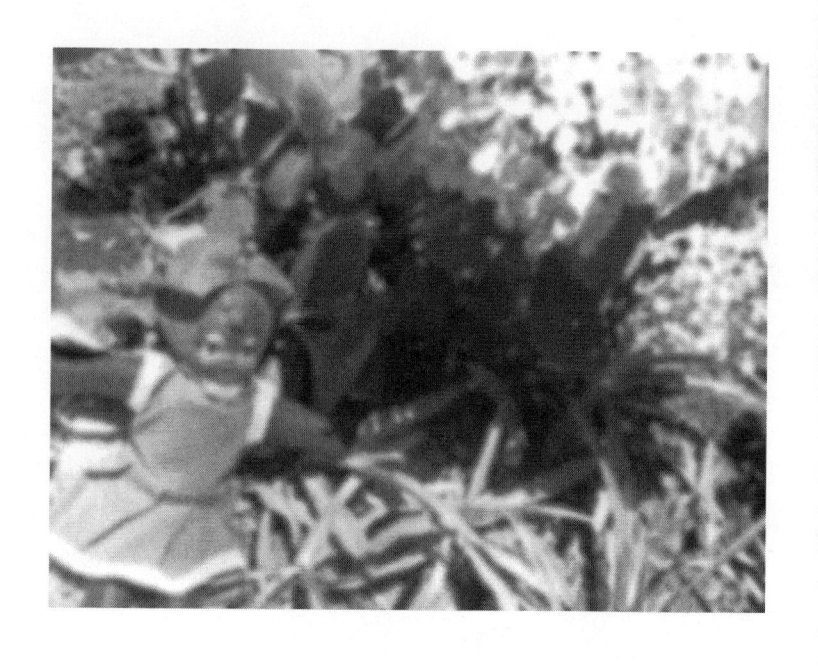

I thought of: my grandmothers, both gone, one from Haiti, one from Alabama; the triangle trade; the third root; Mexican blackness on the legendary small coast; the sensual, exotic body of *la morenita*; the excessive, hidden body of the mammy; the Afro-rhythms of *chilena* music; rap videos; racial loneliness; my singularity and hypervisibility in Mexico; my isolation; my sexual exhibition; my pleasure in my own consumption; eating negritos (cannibalism!); what it means to drink rum. Struggling, I held the doll close. I looked at her from afar. How did we mirror each other? The doll stood at a complicated nexus of feelings and positions; it belonged to a culture not mine, yet literally belonged to me, evoked something of my culture as well. Or gestured somehow towards me. How to judge what she meant in Mexico or what she could mean to me? In the desolate streets of the Distrito Federal, I took pictures of my *muñequita*, my little *negrita* in different public places.

She traveled to the French bakery and sat with yummy croissants. She hung with a mask over her face at a newsstand during the swine flu. She sat on a monument in Parque Mexico. She hung out with kids, played hide-and-seek in a garden. The images started to accumulate into fantasia. I started to materialize her gestures, approximate her ventriloquized voice. What could she say about herself? So blithe and accomplished. I cut up French, Spanish, and English texts, including my curriculum vitae, mash them up and record them on a tape recorder. I have a costume made in her likeness and put it on. I want to turn into her, turn myself into something else. I make a playlist of songs, gather objects, and make dances. I create PowerPoint slides. I have conversations and showings. I want to freak everyone out. I want to figure this out. I design a ritual framework to try and ground everything. I go to Tlaxcala and bring her to life.

Muño (fantasía de la negrita)

(distillation / threshold / new moon ritual)
at the entrance, i stand in an elastic black dress
conforming to my body, a purple straw basket of treasures
and a silver basin at my feet

> from the basket, i pull out a brand new bottle
> of negrita rum: transparent, white

>>> in the background, these songs:
>>> "shirk"—meshell ndegeocello
>>> "you go to my head"—billie holiday
>>> "i know who you are"—björk

muñeca –   1. parte del cuerpo humano.
               2. juguete en forma de figura de mujer o de niña

muñir –   convocar a una junta u otro acto semejante
               sin. amañar, manejar, preparar, disponer,
               manipular, arreglar, apañar
               (*diccionario de la lengua española*)

translation: to summon, call, convoke
               (*cassell's spanish–english dictionary*)

    muño   *muñeca*   *moon*   *yo*

I summon – I call - I convoke

i open the bottle and pour a libation to the ancestors
i move the bottle in the air to the four corners
i cup my right hand and pour rum into it and drink
i cup my left hand and pour rum and let it fall into the basin
i set down the bottle and rub my rum-washed hands together
i summon the public
i take each person, cup their hands, and pour rum into them
    they can drink it or let it fall
    they enter the space

(invocation)
black out. lights up.
i walk from the doorway to the stage
        the purple straw basket on my arm
        the silver basin on my head
i am singing a song from my maternal grandmother
        "jesus loves me this I know"
if the rum ritual was haiti, this song is african-america
        both my legacy
i stop on stage, set down the basin and the basket
        pour more rum into the basin
i open another bottle of rum, salute the four corners
        and begin to pour again

instead of white rum, black Mexican coffee emerges
its smell mingles with the smell of the rum
a projection of the negrita brand rum label appears behind me
i make a magic circle of coffee around the silver basin of rum
i speak in Spanish—part memorized lines, part improvisation

aqui està Performagia	here is Performagia
magia	magic
yo soy magia	l am magic
la gente me dice que soy magia	people tell me I'm magic
yo soy negra	l am a black woman
magia negra	black magic woman

    i dance on the wide circle of coffee grounds,
      slip sliding, intoning in my strange Spanish
    Estaba buscando mi abuelita
        I was looking for my grandmother
  Estaba buscando mi abuelitita
          I was looking for my grand-grandmother
Estaba buscando mi abuelita / y ya no está
        I was looking for my grandmother / she's not there
Estaba buscando mi abuelita
            I was looking for my grandmother . . . .

        en el DF
        en Veracruz
        en Oaxaca
        en Tijuana
        a la frontera
        en Tlaxcala
        en la luna
        en la tierra

Estaba buscando mi abuelita
I was looking for my grandmother
        y ya no está
        she's not there
En lugar, yo encontré la Negrita
instead, I found the Negrita

(transformation)
the projection changes to "*muño* (fantasía de la negrita)"
from the purple basket comes an old-fashioned tape recorder
i press play and you hear my voice
reading a cut-up of the following texts:
"la mujer negra"—nancy morejón
"egotripping"—nikki giovanni
"femme nue, femme noire"—léopold sédar senghor
"who's afraid of aunt jemima"—faith ringgold
"phenomenal woman"—maya angelou
+ lines from my curriculum vitae

e.g. à *l'ombre de ta chevelure / Phenomenal woman / Todavía huelo la espuma del mar que me hicieron atravesar / Anacaona / I am a gazelle so swift / It's in the reach of my arms / La noche no puedo recordarla / with a packet of goat's meat / Concentration in Comparative Literature (High Honors) / Bajo su sel sembré, recolecté y las cosechas no comí. / the span of my hips, / "whisper (the index of suns" / traídos a ella, o no igual que yo." etc. etc. etc.*
                a collision of heritage, a chrysalis of identity

while this plays, i take off the elastic black dress, show skin
i pull from the purple basket, la Negrita's dress
i let it stand on its own crinoline for a minute
before slowly putting it on
i zip myself up from the back
i pull out her shoes one by one, bend over, and put them on
i shake out two scarves and tie them together on my head
with deliberation, i find myself in her body,
or rather, my body in her
i outstretch my hands and close them into fists
i discover myself

< la negrita ya está >

the projection changes again
to a series of slides of la negrita doll in the world.
la negrita at the parque mexico in el distrito federal
at a newsstand wearing a cubraboca. in a french bakery
in tlaxcala in front of the cathedral

> The chilena song "el negro de la costa"
> by pepe ramos begins to play

la Negrita does a happy doll dance!
la Negrita lays in wait!
la Negrita gives hugs!
(la Negrita takes care of the chirren!)
la Negrita hunts for food!
la Negrita considers the Negrito in her pocket!
will she eat it, indulge her cannibal tendencies?
(. . . it's not enough—it's not enough . . .)
la Negrita encounters / reenters the sacred circle

estaba buscando mi abuelita
I was looking for my grandmother
mi abuelitititi teeeeeeeth
my gran gran gran motheeth teeeeeeth

estaba buscando   I was looking
estaba buscando   I was looking
estuve buscando   I did looking
estoy buscando   I am looking

yo busco mi abuelita la negrita
I look for my grandmother the negrita
una negrita, muñequita,
a negrita, a little doll (with moon)

estaba buscando mi abuelita
pero yo encontré
but l found
muñequita, mooooooooooon
a little moon doll, moooooooooooon
yo encontré la muñequita, la negrita
l found my little doll, a negrita
yo muño
l summon—l convoke—l call
mi abuelita la negrita y yo
my grandmother la negrita and me

i pick up the silver basin and pour the rum over my head
it falls over my body. over my costume, seeps into my skin
i place the empty silver basin over my head
i outstretch my arms, close my hands to fists.

"I am the Bird of the Wayside
The sudden scampering in the undergrowth
Or the trunkless head
Of the shadow in the corner."
    —Ama Ata Aidoo
    The Dilemma of a Ghost

(Montreal: Black Women on Walls)

I

Montreal is a city of street art, graffiti, head long in your vision, in the corner of your eyes.

This graffiti, while ubiquitous, does not feel specific to this place. It doesn't shout out gangs or rally political protest.

It is nostalgic but not of the Québec Liberation Front
or other things of this place.
It is coded, but the code is more global than local.
Here, graffiti is a fashion statement.
One that could be in Tokyo or Copenhagen or LA.
One that presumably started as something else,
in 1980s New York, when black and Latino kids wrote on trains,
making graffiti a mark of urban defiance, resistance,
a tenet of hip hop art.
Or so says the lore.
Everywhere, layered tags, spectral street writing.

In this calm and quiet city, graffiti is edgy decoration.
It is innocuous subversion, recognizable global hip hop style.
Here, it says, is our street culture, our urban life,
our underground, our pretty transgression.
This is Montreal, global hip hop city.

What does it mean to have the underground so close to the surface?
What does it mean for this writing to be both so specific and generic?
Once a mark of particular protest, it now feels like an urban brand ...

2

And where is the body in this?
Where is race, both evoked and elided?
Intimated and evacuated in graffiti, where is my black woman's body?

Look at this woman next to the "Vente" or "For Sale" sign.
Is she also for sale or what comes after?
Her body exploded into tags below a Xeroxed face.

She doesn't have to be read as black, and yet, I do.
She makes me think of Joan Collins in *Island in the Sun*,
the white version of a passing redbone gal.
The hair makes me think of my mother in the sixties,
as does the set of the chin. Maybe you would need to be black
to read blackness in this. Those hooded eyes.
Maybe you would need to be me.
Curious, intent, I walk the streets of Montreal,
searching for community, finding evacuated sameness, traces.

3

I am in Montreal at the start of a year of travel.
I am in Montreal writing about performance, identity, and the body.
It is the second week of September, and I am in Montreal,
thinking about memory and location.
What is in the world? Where do I want to be?
I am walking in the world as a black woman traveler.

I am looking for my Haitian people, exiles like my father,
the doctors and teachers and engineers,
who made good in this New World.
The ones who survived the chilly racism
of the Great White North,
the pure race politics of the Liberation Front.
The ones who made it and survived.
I am looking for a particular Haitian woman poet
as well, one whose words I've read over and over
and brought into translation
into my body and performance.
The scuttlebutt in New York says she is here.
I encounter absence, strange traces, ghosts.

On the way to the museum of art, I see this image in a parking lot in Montreal. Blaxploitation woman, looking wistfully up to the sky. Her afro, the curve of her hip, the roundness of her breast all mark the era of nubile black power. Decorative and beautiful, she is a softened version of black political protest.
Warily, she looks away. She does not gaze back.

Or is she rolling her eyes? What do the city denizens see
when they see her, see me, walking down the street?
A soul sign, a throwback, or just another image in the landscape?
Is this her city or is she thinking of another homeland,
the place where she most belongs?
Or does she belong here as much as anywhere else?
This stencil arrives from post-black imagination,
a global hip hop that belongs everywhere and nowhere at once.
Hypervisible and invisible, in Montreal . . .

4

I walk through the city, explore and navigate public space.
I sit at a fountain. I am the only black woman around.
A drunk white man comes up and hassles me.
He won't leave me alone, so I leave.
The next day, I go and sit in a public square.
There is one other black woman there across the park.
A white man approaches and starts to talk to me.

He wants to pick me up but seems strung out or crazy.
I look around. Other women are there.
Both times, the men came up to me.
These experiences don't ruin Montreal for me.
It is still a pretty city of bread and hot chocolate and French.
It is a place for me to explore, to search for signs of black women.
I do yoga in French (*libérez vos corps! sentez vos esprits!*),
take four or five dance classes—tango, modern, African—
in the course of a week.

I want to feel my body in Montreal,
I want to be fully inside it as I experience the city.
The experiences with these men in public places
are other experiences of body.
They are not pleasant experiences, but they aren't unfamiliar either.
They are the wages of a global hip hop city—a place where
ciphers of black women displace the city's imagination.
Those men mistake me for that other woman, the projection
of their desire. Their desire scrawled over everything . . .

5

At my rundown bed and breakfast, I talk to Yolande,
the Haitian cleaning lady. She has heard about my search
for the Haitian poet and knows about Haitians in the city.
Norman, the hotel owner, gets me telephone numbers to call.
I speak with women on phones—Haitian women, black women
who try to lead me to different parts of the city.

The secretary at the Caribbean publishing house tells me
there's no information about the poet I'm seeking.
Another woman from a different community agency tells me:
That woman isn't Haitian. She doesn't really know.
Make sure to talk to the man. He can help you. And he does.
By the end of our conversation, I have the poet's telephone number
and know where she is—although I discover she isn't there.
Despite what I'd heard, she has never lived in Montreal.
Still, I have found her.

The different layers of being in a body in a city.
The circulation of a body inflected by origin.
Black women present even in their absence.

6

Later, I take the subway to another part of town.
I have plans to meet the Haitian writer J.J. Dominique
for coffee and dessert. I am excited to be meeting this woman
whom I so greatly admire. Maybe she can tell me more
about this city, my poet, and the Haitians here.
I get off at a library full of people of color on computers.
I see brown children and families moving through zones
of crowded buildings. Is this their Parisian banlieue?

No cars on fire, but I do see graffiti here as well.
Not as much, though, at least at first sight.
And the black women I see here are real.
J.J. is gracious, and when we sit, we talk about writing
and politics and dance and the city. She tells me that
she lives not too far away, and she likes it because in public
you can hear children, families speaking many different languages.
Not just French or Joual or English but Vietnamese, Kreyòl,
Thai, and Czech. Our conversation gives me hope
for the future of the new global city, new emigrants,
new languages, and maybe new forms.
Maybe new images and writing can come from here.
In this space, where will the black women be?

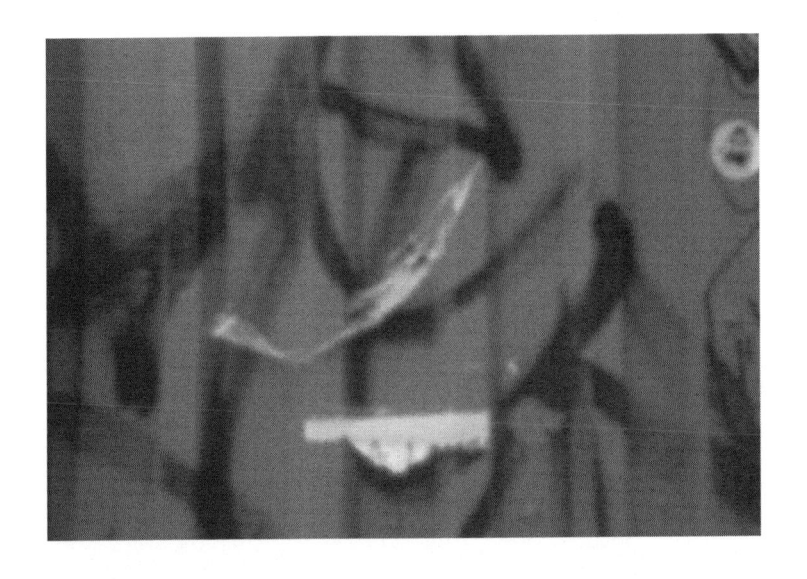

I see this image in Montreal.
It makes me think of the future and the past.
It reminds me of "A Sign in Space,"
one of my favorite stories by Italo Calvino.
The erasure of a sign results not in its absence
but in a sign overlaid by erasure.
Something there, something that covers and reveals
something that used to be there, that is still there somehow,
but also, has slipped away.

This could be poetry, identity, body, presence, future possibility . . .
What will the soul signs of the future be? What body will be there?
What, now abstracted, will be renovated into something else?

7

My last night in Montreal, I go see DJ Krush.
He is a global hip hop DJ par excellence.
He plays it deep and soulful, mainly instrumental mixes, lots of beats.
I spy a few other blacks in the crowd, hanging, bobbing their heads.
To my left, two black women with a black guy.
Maybe even more were at the back. I like to stand in the front.
I like to see the DJ's fingers on the decks.
Krush is a petite Japanese guy in a cargo cap.
He likes to build a mood and spin up to a crescendo.
The majority of the crowd in the front is young, white men.
They stand with their fists balled into their pockets,
their eyes alternately closed or behind cameras, taking shots of Krush.

Behind the DJ were projections.
You already know what they are.
Black women in afros, cool soul dudes from the 1970s.
Black power women, blaxploitation divas.
Soul sisters of the black woman I saw in the lot.
Again and again, in graffiti, in videos,
in translated, imported, global hip hop,
this is what precedes me.
This is what remains after I've gone, is reproduced, repeats.
As a black woman traveler, I arrive already circumscribed.

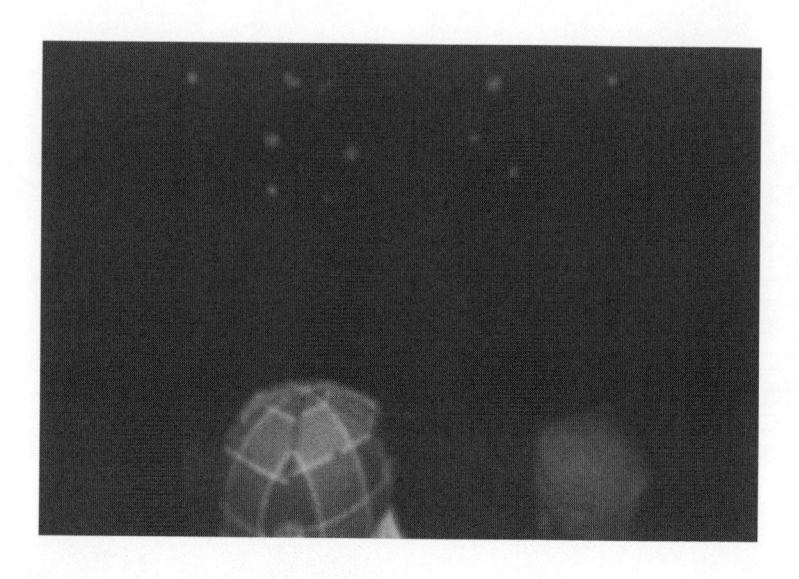

I take this picture from the floor.
You could say it didn't come out—
or maybe it shows what you most need to see.
Unseen in the blackness, the DJ is smiling, taking a picture of us.
The flip side of the tag world of Montreal.
Black women seeing blackness, obscured,
the underground, an open secret.

the queen

Anacaona

Who was Anacaona? Can we ever know? A Taino leader of what is now Haiti and the Dominican Republic, Anacaona, the golden flower, mutates, proliferates, vaporizes in the ether. Start a Google search and see: anacaona song / anacaona boutique hotel in anguilla / anacaona cheo feliciano / anaconda movie. See how the search engine turns her into a snake when she was the one who suffered treachery. Keening toward Caribbean performance, I turn to Haitian playwright Jean Métellus' 1986 play *Anacaona*. Here, she is a beautiful, doomed queen, alarmed by the incursions of the Spanish and rightfully suspicious of them. When their emissaries approach her, she refuses again and again.

Finally, Ovando, a new governor, comes to win her over. He tells her that Queen Isabella in Spain is appalled by the actions of Columbus and his men. The Spanish Queen wants new peace for the island and wants to recognize Anacaona formally as royalty. He implores Anacaona to receive him and she is thrilled with this possibility. Anacaona imagines her heirs mingling with Isabella's heirs for a shared glorious future. The indigenous Queen is no fool. She asks Ovando for hostages as insurance. He complies, and so, she sets out an opulent reception, full of the richest food, the most luxurious drinks. To this lavish spread, Ovando brings men armed to the teeth. When questioned, the Spaniards claim their arms are customary dancing attire. They enter the reception, kill everyone, destroy the castle, and burn Anacaona alive.

my working definition of caribbean performance art:

to hunger. to take and consume. to offer. to sacrifice.
to retain. to retch. to feel belly full. to throw it back.
to exhibit oneself. to body as mas. to make before now.
to think as in clamoring into clothes. to deny nostalgia.
to confiscate treasure. to decorate. to order to feast.
to see one's own skin as ordinary time. to flare nostrils.
to err in kindness. to erase. to bloodfish. to scholarship.
to open your body like a stalk. to open your chest like a clock.
to unstalk. to nibble gnaw devour from the inside.
to hang the skin. to talk out the side of the neck.
to talk one thing to talk the other. to decorate the wound.
to eat. to serve. to crawl back in. to burn finally alive

Published in 1986, the year the baby dictator was sent packing, Métellus' *Anacaona* drapes the Queen in rich, dignified language. She speaks the elegant French of my father's generation (the one under the yoke of the papa dictator). History here is linear and tragic, dignified and well-constructed—so different from what I actually believe about phenomenology, how I actually feel things move through time. In the play, Anacaona cries out in suffering when she realizes her demise « Ô Zémès! / Quel est un hôtage? / Quel est un ésclave? Quels sont les mots de cette prophétie ? » ("O Zémès / What is a hostage ? / What is a slave? What are the words of this prophecy?") She dies before she can see herself turned into a tourist hotel or hear us mispronounce her name, the Taino word for golden flower. The link is tenuous, a claim of landscape more than blood. Still, I want a history more than erasure and obliteration. I can never know her, but I want to embody her and bring her back.

Don't let crazy walk through the door, the black ladies used to say. Don't let them soothe you with sweet words, lure you with false promises. *It's a trap! It's a trap! It's a trap!* Don't believe they can love you, see you, recognize your power. But Anacaona did. Why shouldn't she? She was haughty as a queen. (Is it corny to believe in queens at the site of your subjection? Consider corn and indigenous labor. Popcorn and the cultural bomb... Maize and razed identity... Consider chocolate and lard in Janine Antoni's *Gnaw*. Who gnaws and gets gnawed in Caribbean performance art? How do consumption and power forge diaspora identity?) Anacaona tries to celebrate a future which was already her demise. To perform this would attempt to overthrow time. To reconfigure history once more. Anacaona's fatal flaw was not her vanity but her abundant hospitality. This rang a deep bell for me as an artist, as a black woman, as a diaspora daughter. I would implicate everyone, the audience and even myself. I would offer everything I had, and then, have it thrown back in my face.

Anacaona

(entrance)

the crowd arrives to the antechamber confronted by a reception
a table laden with food: cornbread, corncakes, popcorn, rum
and parcha, a pitcher of clear cool water
cheo feliciano's "anacaona" is playing on repeat
the instructions: eat, drink, dance, and prepare
to present yourself and offer tribute to the queen
later, one by one, the audience walks into the queen's room

attached by a red ribbon to an island throne
i stand in wait a bit away from the door, ready to accept tribute
i try to find and hold body memory / mirror gesture
after gaining admission, each person sits, watches, and waits
while a loop of you and i statements plays on repeat:

i have never been more dead or alive

                                        i precede your wars

you bring swords in your clothes

for the dance

                                        you burn me alive

i pull from you

                                           i shut my chest

you dance the slice of my neck

                                    you dance on my bones

i make skeins of you

                         i fling open the door to Africa

you dance the torch of my halls

                                        you replace me

i have you surrounded

                                  you make of your woman

                                          a wood a myth

you dance me burning

                                        i stand before you

you have made of your warriors

a national religion

i allow you

                                              you devour

you make of your poetry a dirge

                                       i recur in a dream

i fail to face history

                                    you make me the land

you devoured your own ancestors

i take you as hostage

you bleed me and make me swim

i offered sweets at the wake

you split me open

i lie

you discover gold kernels

hiding in stalk

you throw it back on my face

i struggle i blur

you mirror me

i cover recover

you refract me from myself

i await your tribute

you misunderstand the dynamics

of our power

i offer you vegetable hospitality

i gnaw

on the screen: the word anacaona *in red*

(walk backwards)
*body memory of gestures moving back into the queen walk clear missteps
and repetitions remember jamaica kincaid: "her heels, only her heels . . .
coming down to meet me forever . . ." i return to my throne, my chair
attached to me with red ribbon and begin to speak:*

(smear gold)
If i tell you   i know Anacaona / then you know that i am lying / russet
skin fleshy eyelids a recurring dream the obvious / a white slip lips
like a flattened heart / if i say / i see Anacaona / red bone almond eyes
lips like a slit / flattened heart a void you know / that i am a strain /
lying men of a certain age / hum an expected salsa / look at my heels
my diadem / something rending can't make / the journey Aye Bombé
Aye Bombé / Africa will come soon the meaning / of her name /
Anacaona flower of gold / *Ils cherchent de l'or de l'or de l'or / Or Or
Or Or Oro Oro Oro* / or if i say anacaona is a / i confess my own lack
named and floating / i smear the standard of history

*still attached to my throne, i start to peel ears of corn
i prepare to address my subjects / my guests
i read or recite or move with the words of prophecy in my head:*

(strange prophecy from métellus)
« Pourquoi voulez-vous que nous
vous rassemblions ? Ne suis-je
pas, de votre avis même, reine
d'un royaume prospère ?
Entourée du matin au soir des plus
beaux objets jamais sortis de
main d'homme Louée comme
Reine ainsi que Bohéchio l'était
Et possédant, encore, malgré
vos frères, un palais regorgeant de
chefs d'œuvres, de calebasses
ciselées ou peintes, d'étoffes
teintes de vives couleurs de
sièges souples et légers, de
hamacs aériens, de fabuleux
éventails, de masques ornés d'or,
de parures en coquillages,
de pierres sculptées et de chaises

(simultaneous prophecy)
voiced over on a tape:
a bow. an entrance
fit for a queen body.
memory. anacaona hauteur
and some flesh.
smear gold and tender
resignation. peel stalk.
field prophecies. failing
gods. market analysis.
currency of dreams.
we see them skin less.
moon faced. they see her.
them. more dear. she sees
her self. a monarchy
of memory. tabula raza
primitiva. a mother
with three legs. nostalgia.

de repos, comme mon duho,
taillées dans une seule pièce
de gaïac et imitant un animal
appuyé sur quatre pattes. Ne
nous trouvez-vous pas
suffisamment élevés en esprit ?

languor. a womb. always
a shield. a shawl of green.
naked bundle of partial
songs. boiled corn. nerves. skin. to
order. to hostess.
to serve. to crawl back in

(shuck corn)
the queen is hungry, so i peel the corn and as a kind of aside
begin to speak, and then bite into the corn and eat
do y'all know the bahamian performance artist janine antoni?
she gnawed a giant block of lard and one of chocolate
she cut a backpack out of a cow skin that she hung and stretched
she filmed her boyfriend licking her eye
she displays a monstrous appetite
anyway, she has one photograph i love
very poised very west indian a parlor
with curtains that contain the light

a couch or chair stiff as if made for this holding
her mother sitting skin light pale as if
she'd walked under a sun umbrella her whole life
her face is placid and correct, but when you look
closer you see that she has three legs, her daughter,
the artist crouches up under her, trying to crawl back in
so many ways to look for anacaona
so many ways to find her devouring and skinning
elaborate and sturdy display, the third leg and the stiff chair and
the cow eye and the lard before burning gnaw

(let's have a party!)
¡ Préparons des festins inoubliables
une petite soirée ! / here's how to do it:
gather three hostages, tell them:
cross your fingers behind your back
stand and make the sign of the crossed

fingers behind your back
then promise never to betray me
i pass around a big basket of popcorn
kernels & candy corn & ribbons saying:
i know what you want take it fill your pockets you know you want it
c'mon but haven't you already danced and eaten i know what you
want and you greedy you've already had your party you've already
danced to the sound of the wake you take my hospitality go ahead
lift it up in your hands feel my bounty
and abundance taste it popping open in your mouth in your hands
<u>and throw it back at me</u>

(hospitality in default)
you thought you were something, black girl?
cringe wince shudder shake recoil
get down off your high horse! pathetic pelted in defeat

                                        miles davis'
                             "sketches of spain" begins to play

(sketches of spain)
i scramble to grab kernels from the floor
i try to put it all in my mouth and swallow
i feel more acutely the ribbon attaching me to the chair
i seek the machete
it needs to be cut
i need to be cut
i need to be cut free
i find the machete
turn to someone there
implore command
CUT ME LOOSE

(somehow what happens)
the shell and the fan
the cause and effect
the show and the scheme
the afterparty and the aftermath
the hubbub and hullabaloo
the shame and the rebuke
the chewed corn in my mouth
the now spit on the ground
the shoulda known better
the nobody cares
the loss and dereliction
the revocation and return
the shame on you
the impossible herstory
the trying to shine
the bloodlust
the i lost control
the body memory
the holding back of tears
the new world now

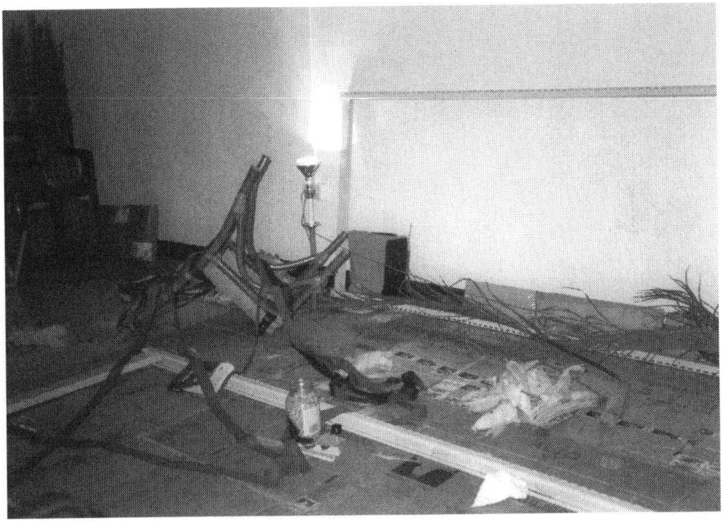

(all the spanish I know)
in Jean Métellus' *Anacaona*, the queen doesn't speak
Spanish at all which is good because I don't speak
Spanish at all / here's all the Spanish I know . . .

>
> *ahora*
> *barco*
> *calor*
> *dónde*
> *época*
> *frío*
> *garganta*
> *hora*
> *izquierda*
> *jacaranda*
> *k . . .*
> *labio*
> *mañana*
> *naufragio*
> *oscuro*
> *poder*
> *quiero*

> *suspendida*
> *total*
> *uva*
> *x (a kiss)*
> *yo*
> *zoo . . .*

(Ô Zémès)
in Jean Métellus' *Anacaona*, the queen wrings her hands
when she hears the news of her demise, she calls her dead god
Ô Zémès Ô Zémès Ô Zémès
¿ What is a hostage ? ¿ What is a slave ?
¿ What are the words of this strange prophesy ?

"boooooooo. spooky ripplings of icy waves, this
umpteenth time she returns—this invisible woman
long on haunting short on ectoplasm . . .

as she strives to retrieve flesh to cloak her bones
again to thrive to keep her poisoned id alive.
useta be young useta be gifted—still black"

      —Wanda Coleman
      "American Sonnet (35)"

(Detroit: Black Parties & Spirit)

There has to be food and drink, drinks and music, and you need to be able to wear your shoes inside because sometimes your shoes are the best part of your outfit. Teetering high heels or hard black boots or sneakers straight out the box. A party makes your shoes dancing shoes. And the height of a party is dancing. Kick back, kick up your heels. Make merry, make light, take flight, flow. Celebrate and savor. Simmer into crescendo. A volume of voices, loud or low, it's all good as long as you hear a hum of pleasure, a crackle of satisfaction.

    This comes to me by blood.

Haitian children dressed in the frilliest dresses, yellow and pink and sky blue, or in tiny suits with jackets and ties, accompanying their immigrant parents to a fête. Or on the other side, at a barbecue with chicken and beer, listening to soul. Down in the basement, my parents in the '60s in Detroit mingling these two strains with family and friends. One group just off the boat and the other not too far from the cotton field. The way they moved with Caribbean flavor, Southern warmth, and Motown soul, there had to be some Africa in there too . . . Right? They would dance all night until six in the morning, the children secretly jumping on the bed upstairs until they fell asleep in heaps.

People swallowed fire at those parties, walked on glass.

My mother and godmother in their new, slick falls. My father, my godfather, my uncle, all clean-shaven, looking sharp as a tack. My cousin Ghislaine dancing hard to "Guantanamera" in the center of the floor. Boule-da-fee in another spot doing the same. I saw Boule at a Haitian New Year's function a few years ago. With grey hair and a walker, he was still throwing down.

And those nights at those parties, women did the spirit dance, ran forward and thrust out their chests, and then ran back, a dance black women have been doing for centuries.

Wiggling, twisting, grinding, holding onto their men, holding onto each other, letting go, catching up, getting free, getting up, getting down, doing their best to get to glory.

A party is a conjuring of magical space, an invitation, an offering, a remembering. Flushed and pulsing, together, they silently cajoled: *bring this here / bring this back / keep this here / bring us back / bring us here / bring us back / to this.*

the ghost

ghost / gesture

I am writing this from the back of a taxi in Dakar—
my driver is decked out in flowing white.
Today is Friday—Muslim holy day, and I feel
well rested and delighted to be here.
      It is 11:15 AM, and I'm already heading to the airport
to be there at 2 PM to take a 5:30 PM flight to Banjul,
and that will take all of 30 minutes.
At first, the idea of all this time was maddening—
but now I feel relaxed and excited. I'm looking out
at ocean and dirt and sand and trees and cement
blocks, and I do feel more grounded. Having caught up
on sleep helped a lot. I slept from 4 AM,
when I arrived at the hotel to 11 AM and then from 4 to 9 PM,
and then again, from 11ish to 8 AM—the difference is amazing.
I don't want to meet Rosa cranky, and I also feel
that clear purpose is crucial to thinking through
and planning + rehearsing + making the performance.

    And so, this morning,
to awake well rested
to put on a little luminizer
to go and buy croissants at a bakery (thinking it was a café)
to walk down the street and find another café
to insist on an orange table near a window
to chat in French!
to see men in their Friday finery and beaux boubous
to see women elegant and lovely
to drink a café au lait
to walk down the street and ogle elegant shoes
to then indulge myself in a bookstore + buy an Assia Djebar novel
(I know it should have been Senegalese)
to wallow in the being here: the Motherland!

Something about African frequency. Air space.
From the moment I was heading into the continent,
the way things changed. In the airport in Casablanca,
on the way to Dakar. How the dial turned—
static became crackle and the older women
bedecked in their fine crowns
pushed me out of the way in line.
Why should I stand before them
on the way back home?

If we all emit a frequency, picked up variously
at different places in the world, I am somehow
being picked up here. Literally.
Barry from Guinée-Konakry on the plane,
helping me change money, splitting a cab, and walking
me around town the next day. Or even on the way from the hotel
to the airport once more, to complete my whirlwind tour to
meet Rosa in Banjul: Detroit-New York-London-Barcelona
(where I was so exhausted and uncomfortable in the airport,
I paid 50 euros to go sleep for 3 hours in a hotel—the most
expensive nap of my life)-Casablanca-Dakar—and then,
an interruption.

Just as I was settling down with my book for an afternoon
in an airport, Oumar approaches. Are you waiting here long?
he asks. Not too long, I say with American wariness.
Look, the airport is boring. Let me show you around.
(*And who was this black girl who would go off
with an unknown African guy pre-cell phone
on only her second full day on the continent?
Oh right, that's me.*) Sensing my wavering,
he pulls out his ID card. This is who I am.
The guys here know me and can vouch for me.
Je suis une personne bon-bon.

And so, we're off—to see the sea, to watch fishermen unload
a fresh catch, and to pay for one fish to be split and roasted for us
on the spot. There's a plan for me to return to Dakar
and do a performance. He tells me he drums.
He can get a group of friends together to be my backing band.
He's a hustler but could maybe become a friend.
This is Dakar. (Rosa says African men have *lyrics*.)

Hours later, I sit in a hammock in The Gambia, the sun on my face, the same sea on my right, and Rosa working at a table on my left. I've been basking in African adventures, but now, it's time to work on this show.

From the beginning, that desire for ghosts . . .
(*How to return to a place where you've never been?*
Well, of course, you must be a ghost . . .)
And what do I know of this world?

ghost / gesture

(*elements*)
a black woman's body returned
white sheets, mound of sand
1-2 silver pots, flour, water
4-5 stones, rolls of white paper
a long rope of black and red synthetic braided hair
a small hand mirror

(*set space*)
The performance takes place in a nightclub during the day.
The performance space is partially encircled by low stone walls
studded with mirrors. In the center of the space stands a roll
of white paper rooted in a mound of local sandy dirt.
Around this white paper, which looks like a fat votive candle,
stand two silver pots and four stones set in the four directions.
On far ends of the space, stand two other rolls of white paper.

(*The Spook Who Sat by the Door*)
She sits near the entrance, wrapped in a white sheet dress.
Isn't that the proper attire for a ghost?
She looks at the door, her body subtly keening
at any oncoming presence.
Her people arrive. Music plays for their procession.

> "I am not Seaworthy"—Kathleen Battle & André Previn
> Libretto by Toni Morrison
> "Submarine"—Björk (*"to return / do it now.*
> *Shake us out of the heavy deep sleep.*
> *Shake us now. Do it now."*)

(*Middle Passage*)
She rolls her sheeted body. Stands. Moves backwards.
Unfurls another white sheet. Spreads it in air.
Shakes it out onto the floor. Her body rolls, folds, rocks

into the sheet. Triangulated. Her body. In this sheet.
The sheet becomes a boat. She is becoming engulfed.
Is only a leg visible? The crook of an arm.
The boat of her body moving across the floor.
Diaphanous. Veiled and kneeling. Unveiling, rising.
Bluish white shades in the dark light. Her body,
a blackness, like the light.

(*The Ghost Speaks*)
How to return if you've never been?
Poetry in phantasm. Body X-ray. Apparition.
Ghost / Gesture
Will I be white?
Will I be transparent?
Will I eat fish or just the bones?
Will I be able to walk through walls?
Will I be able to see through walls?
Will you be able to see me?
Will you be able to touch me?
Will you know me then?
(*The sheet of the boat slips away.*)
Do you know me now?
Have you seen the spirits?
Are they here?
(*She waves a piece of her ghost dress in the air.*)

Or do I just want them to be?
When does it start?
Is it ever over?
(She balls up the boat ship into a baby sized ball in her hands.)
What time of day is forever?
What time of night is all white? All the way through?
(She rolls the baby ball away).

>   DJ Soul Slinger's "Who R U" begins to play.

(*Crown/ Braid /Fence*)
She pulls, unwinds from the crown of her head an almost
infinitely long braid of synthetic hair, interwoven tresses
of black and red. She ties one end to a chair nearby
and walks through the space, unwinding, moving the braid
through the space, leaving traces of synthetic hair.
She dances with the braid like a rope, a whip.

At first, she does this in silence.
But then she speaks again.

(*Casper*)
When I think of a ghost, I think of Casper,
the friendly ghost. I think of the Holy Ghost
in Christianity. And I think of myself
>   here
>   now.

(She continues unraveling the giant braid.
Moving her body with it, laying it down as a fence,
a boundary around the ritual space in the center.)
How can you return if you've never been?

(*Body X-ray*)
Around the center piece of paper, pots and stones,
she creates a circle with the giant braid.

She picks up a pocket mirror,
the shape of a rectangle in her hands.
She scans the air around her
walking the length of the audience, the circle of the space.
She scans each row of the audience with care.
She then scans her own body, running the mirror from
the tip of each foot up each leg, over her neck and her face.
She does not scan the whiteness of her ghost dress.
She asks:
Don't you sometimes wonder what happened?
Then.
Afterwards.
Haven't you ever wondered what it would be like
to come back? Or to never be able to leave?
Or am I the only one?
But I don't think so . . .
She scans the ritual space, the length of braid,
the roll of paper that looks so much like a fat white candle,
the pots, the stones. She sets the X-ray mirror down by the
stone wall studded with mirrors. Is it home?

(*Paper Armature*)
She walks to a corner, runs, and unrolls
a long white sheet of paper across the back of the floor.
She walks to another corner, runs and unfurls
another long sheet of paper. The sheets of paper together
make a V across that space that she crosses / passes over.
At each end, she rips paper away from the roll.
She wraps paper around her. It becomes a stole,
an armor, a ghost armature for the ritual end.
What was fabric before has now become paper.
She curls paper around her body, stuffs paper into her dress,
pads herself with paper, something not soft,
something not quiet. The crunchand rustle of paper is the only sound.
Unsettling, she keeps wrapping herself in paper
until she is more than cocooned:

She is straitjacketed by paper.
She kneels before the audience,
picks up a silver pot and anoints herself,
not with paper, but with water. On her feet. On her face.
She picks up another silver pot and anoints herself
not with paper, not with water, but with flour.
It sprinkles first, then showers.
Her body keeps moving backward,
back toward the door.
A little more. A little more.
Eruption. Clatter.
Rattle of bones. Cloud of dust.
The ghost throws the silver pot
of flour all over body and runs out:

an apparition of white sheet
white flour white paper
brown flesh
she disappears
 into the sun
(and returns   )

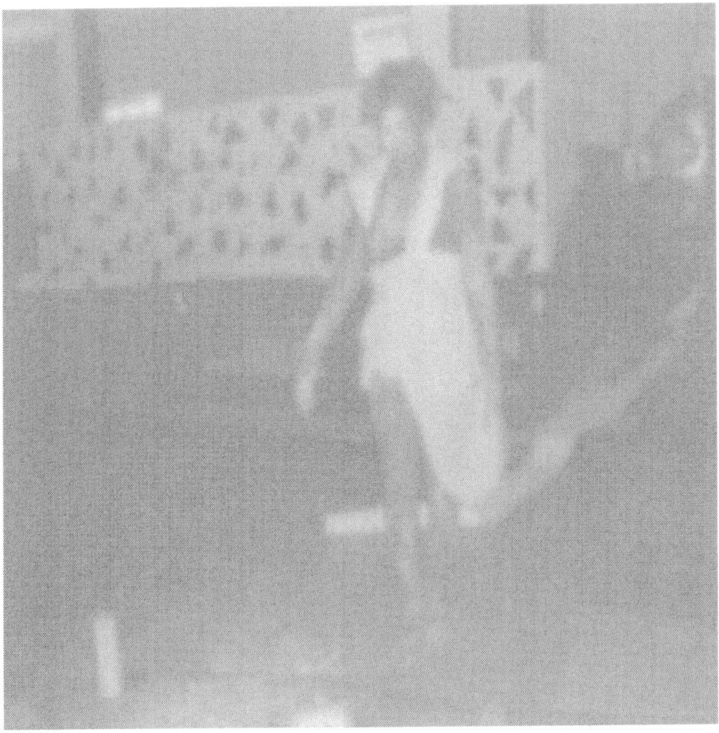

Muño (fantasía de la negrita) took place in Tlaxcala, Mexico in 2009.
Anacaona took place in Río Piedras, Puerto Rico in 2003.
ghost / gesture took place in Banjul, The Gambia in 2006.

The performance text of Muño appeared in the Performagia 7 festival catalogue edited by Pancho López, 2011.

"Anacaona: Notes toward Caribbean Performance Art" appeared in *Sargasso: Journal of Caribbean Theater and Performance,* Special Issue on the NEH Seminar on Caribbean Theater & Performance, 2004-2005.

Frontispiece and back page illustration by the author. All photos were taken by the author except for the photos of *Anacaona* and *ghost/gesture*, which were taken by Rosamond S. King.

Special thanks to Rosamond S. King for performance witness and solidarity. Thanks to Bhanu Kapil, Muriel Leung, Marcus Clayton, Kenji C. Liu, Gold Line Press, and all my ancestors, ghosts, family, and friends.

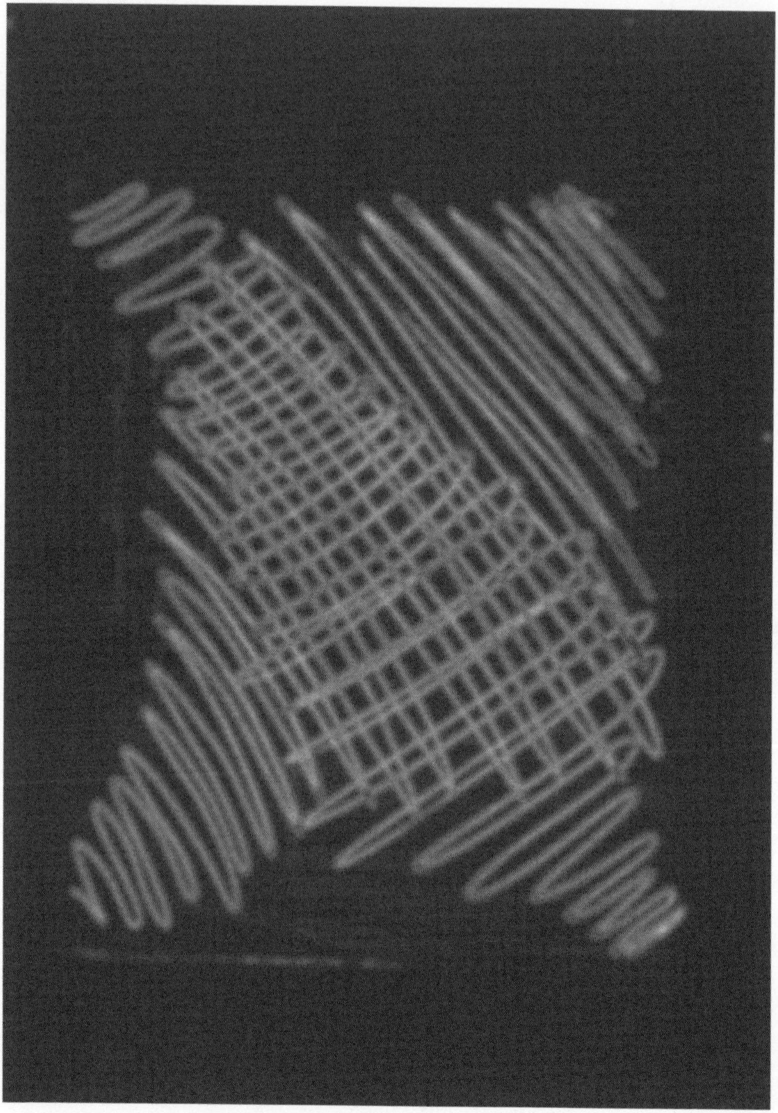

GABRIELLE CIVIL is a black feminist performance artist, poet, and writer, originally from Detroit, MI. She has premiered fifty original performance art works around the world including in Puerto Rico, The Gambia, Ghana, Canada, Zimbabwe, and Mexico where she lived as a Fulbright Fellow. She is the author of the performance memoirs *Swallow the Fish* (2017) and *Experiments in Joy* (2019). A 2019 Rema Hort Mann LA Emerging Artist, she teaches creative writing and critical studies at the California Institute of the Arts. The aim of her work is to open up space.